[1] **The Genealogy of Christ**
Detail: Jesus Christ
(inner narthex, fourth bay, southern dome)

[1]

Saint Saviour in
CHORA

Fatih Cimok

A TURİZM YAYINLARI

HISTORICAL BACKGROUND

The tradition which claims the existence of a church or monastery of any kind before the construction of the land walls of Theodosius II (408–50) in 413 is thought to have derived from the topographical interpretation of the meaning of the word *chora*. The word and its cognates, *choros* and *chorion*, refer to land, country, a suburb or suburban area, or a country town. By the fourteenth century it had become the custom to dedicate a church to Christ and the Virgin, and define it with mystical qualities such as the Akataleptos (incomprehensible), Dynamis (all-powerful), Evergetes (benefactor), Pantokrator (omnipotent); the Virgin being defined as the Eleousa (merciful), Pammakaristos (all-blessed) or Panachrantos (all-pure). Even if it was not true for the earlier church, chapel or monastery which might have existed in the same area, the present edifice which was repaired and enlarged by Theodore Metochites was, in accordance with the custom, dedicated to Christ and the Virgin as the *chora*, the land, sphere, or dwelling-place of the living, and the dwelling-place of the uncontainable (God), respectively. Thus the original word has survived to the present in its new context, as in St Martin's in the Fields or St Germain des Près.

The structural history of the first building constructed on the same spot in the early seventh century is complex and beyond the interest of the ordinary visitor. Like many other monasteries of the Byzantine Empire it must have fallen into poverty during the period of Iconoclasm, until 843 when it was restored. From this period until the last quarter of the eleventh century, there is no information concerning the monastery.

THE FIRST KOMNENE CHURCH

The historian Nikephoros Gregoras provides the only document regarding the construction of this, the first Komnene church. Although he was a historian of the later period Nikephoros was a protégé of Theodore Metochites, lived in the monastery of the Chora, and was intimately connected with it. In his *Byzantina Historia*, he narrates that the church of the Chora 'had been built in ancient times by the Emperor Justinian . . . time having destroyed . . . [Justinian's church] to its foundations, the mother-in-law of the Emperor Alexius [I] Komnenos had another church erected from its foundations, in the form in which it is now seen, but inasmuchas time was again threatening to destroy it, . . . [Theodore Metochites], with a lavish hand, beautifully restored everything except the innermost naos'.

If the words of Nikephoros Gregoras about the first church, which are derived from a dubious source which has no historical value, are left aside, he speaks of two phases of construction: the new church of the mother-in-law of Alexius I Komnenos (1081–1118), and its restoration by Theodore Metochites. The first founder, the mother-in-law of the Emperor Alexius I Komnenos, had played a prominent role in the affairs of the Dukas and Komnenos families over a particular period. Her edifice dates from the years between 1077 and 1081. It was thought to have been a building of the 'four-column' type which was very popular in the eleventh century.

THE SECOND KOMNENE CHURCH

The church of Maria Dukaena did not last long, and probably because of the slipping of the foundations on the east side, fell into ruins, and had to be restored. The Deesis panel in the fourth bay of the inner narthex offers a clue about the second Komnene church. In the lower corners of the panel the portraits of two imperial personages are included. The one on the left belongs to Isaak Komnenos, third son of the Emperor Alexius I Komnenos and Irena Dukaena, and grandson of Maria Dukaena, the founder of the first Komnene church. This must have been in the early twelfth century. In the prevailing Byzantine tradition, when a church was refounded it was a custom to commemorate early founders or foundresses, and it seems that Theodore Metochites followed this Byzantine tradition. The portrait at the right of the panel represents the Lady of the Mongols, a relative of the Emperor Andronikos II Palaiologus, There is no evidence to show her connection with the monastery.

The history of the building until it was restored by Metochites is not known. There is no information about whether it was abandoned or continued to function during the Latin occupation (1204–61). However, it must have continued to be used, because of its closeness to the Blachernae Palace.

THE CHURCH OF THEODORE METOCHITES

About two hundred years later a third building project, that of the present monument, was undertaken by Theodore Metochites. The exact date when Metochites became the founder of the Chora and began his restoration is not known. However, the decoration of the church is thought to have been completed by the end of 1320 or the first months of 1321. There are no surviving records or information about the building activities. It is assumed that the rebuilding of the nave, and the addition of the narthexes and the pareclesion took one or two years, and Metochites was not in a position to meet the heavy expenses until 1308. The making of mosaics is a longer process than that of painting frescoes, and it must have taken three years to finish the extensive mosaic decoration of the nave and narthexes. Such estimates suggest that the entire restoration was carried out between 1315 and 1320–21.

When Metochites started his restoration, the dome of the edifice had collapsed but the shell of the nave was left in place. This was a dome of approximately 8 m in diameter, and it rested upon masonry piers, the corners of which projected into the nave. The projecting corners of the piers form a cruciform ground plan with shallow cross-arms. From the dome which Metochites built, only the cornice has survived to the present. At four cardinal points of this there are still four monograms which give his name and titles – east: Theodoros; west: Metochites; south: Logothetes; north: kai Ktetor. The dome of today's building is Ottoman, constructed of timber and covered with plaster.

It is not known for sure whether the marble panels of the nave belonged to the previous revetment and were reset by masons of Metochites in their places, or were newly supplied by himself. They were cut into thin slices and set on the walls like the pages of a book. With the technique of those days, the cutting of marble was a very difficult job. First a groove was chiselled along the top of the block of stone and filled with sand. Two men then cut into it using a cord or blade as though it were a two-handed toothless saw, grinding away the stone with sand. If one knows that in one day only about 5 cm of marble could be cut, one can appreciate the work involved in producing these marble panels. However, after a time, hand-operated saws gave way to saws operated by water power.

Nothing has survived from the furnishing of the bema, and it is not known whether Metochites found it necessary to change these. The excavations of

the Byzantine Institute revealed that under the floor of the apse there was a suitable room for the altar, and the foundations for columns of a ciborium. When the church was transformed into a mosque in 1510 by Atik Ali Paşa, the Grand Vizier of Sultan Bayezit II (1481–1512), a marble 'mihrap' was placed in the apse.

The two narthexes of the Chora were entirely new constructions of Metochites. The inner one is not centred with regard to the nave, and the two domes that cover its end bays are consequently off axis. The outer narthex too, is divided into very unequal bays. The vertical walls and lunettes were constructed of bands of four courses of brickwork alternating with four courses of roughly-dressed stone. The arches and vaults were constructed of brick, and were faced with marble — mainly Prokennesian — and green breccia. Above the cornice where the marble facing ended, the mosaic began.

The mosaics of the Chora are among the rare examples of late Byzantine art that have survived to the present. With the Latin occupation of Constantinople in 1204, most of the Byzantine artists migrated to the Balkans and Russia to search for new patrons for whom they could execute their art. Those who were left in the city had to compromise with the taste of the new patrons. During this period, art forms such as monumental paintings, especially mosaic, ceased to be executed. Icon production, fashionable jewellery and figural sculpture gained new momentum. A process of secularization in art which seems to have begun in the twelfth century was intensified.

With the recovery of the capital in 1261 a large number of artists started returning to Constantinople. More than 50 years had passed, and these were not those who had fled from the city. They were no longer part of an accepted order, held together by established iconographic or stylistic conventions. Some came from Serbia, some from Nicaea. Many of them had never been to Constantinople before. Their outlook and their art was much more personal and individualistic than tha of their fathers. The result was the birth of a new religious art after a period of secularization, with emphasis on a new style. Nevertheless, the result is not always regarded as a 'renaissance'. The taste and outlook were changed but the medieval patterns of mind were not abandoned. For instance to render evil figures such

[3]

as the Devil in scenes of temptation, or King Herod, or soldiers in the Massacre of the Innocents, in profile, was a style. However, in the Chora this rule seems to have been slackened. Secondary figures such as maids or onlookers are shown in profile. In Byzantine art, figures who were drawn from the back did not exist at all. The artists of the Chora seem to have been ignorant of this rule. Among the other oddities there is the ending of drapery in the shape of a hook, and the drawing of naked feet with heavy shadows, as if the figures are wearing sandals without strings. The artists at the Chora give the impression that they simply tried new ways of expression.

The starting point of the iconographic programme of the mosaics in the Chora is the life cycles of the Virgin and Christ. The flutes of the southern and northern domes of the inner narthex where the ancestry of the Virgin and Christ are depicted, serve

as a prelude to these cycles. The major source of the life cycle of Mary, which fills most of the inner narthex, is from the apocryphal Protevangelium of James.

In the Byzantine tradition, to build or restore churches or monasteries was the responsibility of the members of the noble class. When such a foundation or restoration took place the patron was granted the title of 'ktetor', or founder. In the Palaiologian period especially, the church would be regarded as a family church. In such family churches it was normal to portray the founder, to carve his name and initials, and to house his tomb or those of his family members. The church of the Chora fell within the pattern of that tradition. It is very probable that the tomb in the north wall of the second bay of the pareclesion was the tomb of Theodore Metochites.

[4] **The Enthroned Christ and the Donor**
Detail: Theodore Metochites, founder of the
monastery of the Chora

THEODORE METOCHITES

Theodore Metochites (c 1260–1332), founder of the monastery of the Chora, was born in Constantinople. The capital of his time was a small state where everybody knew everybody, wrote to everybody and was related to everybody by marriage. The members of the aristocracy loved books and were thirsty for knowledge. They read, wrote, copied. Metochites was from a wealthy and cultivated family. His father was George Metochites, who was an ardent supporter of the union with the Roman Church. Metochites must have spent a comfortable childhood until his parents were exiled to Asia Minor for the political opinions of his father. There, the young boy continued his interrupted education and went through the 'trivium' (grammar, rhetoric, logic) and 'quadrivium' (arithmetic, astronomy, geometry, music).

Metochites must have understood the importance of education and learning for surviving in Byzantine society, for at an early age he decided to become a scholar – though he ended up becoming a politician. He studied philosophy, sacred books, ancient literature and theology. Before he was 20 he tried his hand at literature and composed exercises of Greek history and eulogies of saints.

His fortune was changed in 1290, when he was brought to the attention of Emperor Andronikos II (1282–1328) who was then visiting Nicaea. He was taken into the service of the Emperor, despite the fact that his father was still in the state prison.

His advancement in the service of the palace was rapid. He was soon granted a court title and membership in the senatorial class. When he was 36 years old he became the prime minister of the Emperor. By giving his daughter to John Palaiologus, the Emperor's nephew, he became related to the imperial family. During these years, while climbing to the summit of success he increased his private fortune as well. By selling offices, land grants, titles and sinecures, he accumulated material wealth second only to that of the Emperor.

In 1316 he started the restoration of the Chora, which was a functioning monastery under the protection of the State, but in poor condition. In his writings Metochites expresses his purpose in the restoration openly: first, to immortalize his name; secondly to serve him as a permanent shelter in his old age – as if he had foreseen approaching events. In the northwestern pendentive of the first bay of the pareeclesion, there is an angel and a small soul who are facing towards the scene of the Last Judgement. It is very probable that this was done on the order of Metochites. In one of his writings Metochites addressed the archangel Michael and asked him to intercede on his behalf during the days of the Last Judgement. To achieve his aims, Metochites used his personal resources and those of the State relentlessly. After restoring the building, he decorated it with mosaics and frescoes. He provided it with a continuous income by assigning it the revenues of some fertile lands and vineyards. Through his efforts, the monastery became a vast enterprise with a public hospital, a public kitchen and its own efficient organization to collect funds from the property it owned. While some of this property was near the capital, some was in far away regions. In addition to its large monastic community, the monastery sheltered monks from Asia Minor and other regions of the Empire, and owned a very large and rich library. In 1321, Metochites was granted the highest court office of his career, that of Grand Logothete, the controller of the state treasury. However, he could not enjoy his wealth and his new office in peace. The civil war which had broken out between Andronikos II and his grandson Andronikos III (1328–41), ended with the victory of the latter. In 1328 the political career of Metochites came to an end. His palace was destroyed, his house was pillaged, his properties and wealth were confiscated, and he was exiled to Didymoteichos in Thrace where he lived until 1330. He was by then a sick old man without any hope or money. He wanted to return to the capital and live in the monastery he had founded, and the canon law provided that the founder of a monastery who had become destitute through no fault of his own had the right to demand support from his foundation. He took monastic vows and became Theoleptos the monk. After spending his last two years in the Chora, he died on 13th March, 1332 and was buried in the pareeclesion of the Chora.

[5]

[5] The drawing of feet with black shadows as if they were clad in sandals with the necessary strings ommitted, is another idiosyncrasy of design often encountered in the mosaics of the Chora.

[6]

[6] One of the curious features of the mosaics and frescoes of the Chora is the little 'tail like' drapery with its upturned end, almost like a hook. It brings to mind a personal signature. The artist of all of these scenes was probably the same person and he wanted to leave his signature on his work.

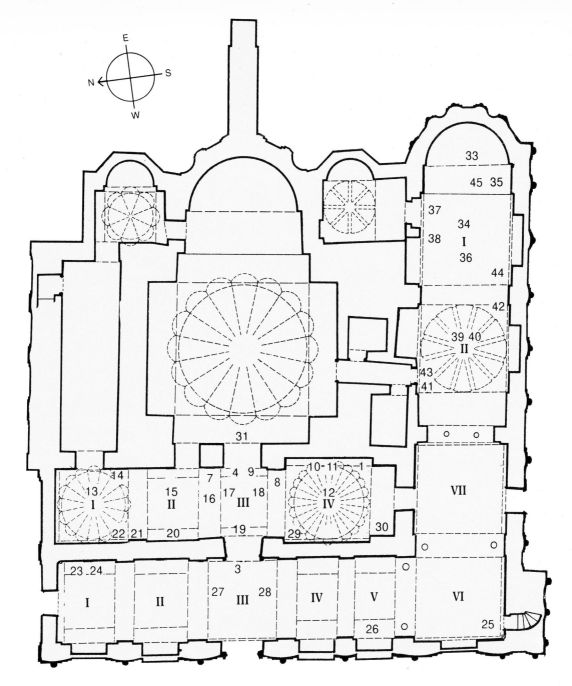

General plan of the Chora and key numbers to the location of the mosaics included in this volume

[1] Jesus Christ
[3] Christ Pantokrator
[4] Theodore Metochites (cover picture)
[7] St Peter
[8] St Paul
[9] The Enthroned Christ and the Donor
[10] The Deesis; the Virgin
[11] The Deesis; Christ Pantokrator
[12] The Genealogy of Christ
[13] The Genealogy of Christ
[14] The Annunciation to St Anne
[15] The Birth of the Virgin
[16] The First Seven Steps of the Virgin
[17] The Presentation of the Virgin in the Temple
[18] The Presentation of the Virgin in the Temple
[19] The Virgin Receiving the Skein of Purple Wool
[20] The Virgin Entrusted to Joseph
[21] Joseph Taking the Virgin to his House
[22] The Annunciation of the Virgin at his House
[23] The Enrolment for Taxation
[24] The Enrolment for Taxation
[25] Herod Ordering the Massacre of the Innocents
[26] The Mothers Mourning for their Children
[27] The Miracle at Cana
[28] The Multiplication of Loaves
[29] Christ Healing Two Blind Men
[30] Christ Healing the Leper
[31] The Dormition of the Virgin

9

[7]

[7] St Peter

Detail: bust
St Peter
(inner narthex, left side of the door leading into the nave)

Of the two saints placed on either side of the entrance to the nave, St Peter is given the more honoured position by being placed to the right of the figure of Christ above. With his right hand he firmly grips the scroll containing his epistles (omitted in the picture). From his upraised left hand two keys – the 'keys of the kingdom of heaven' – hang from the ends of a short cord. His himation is rendered in yellow, which is his colour in the mosaics and frescoes of the Chora.

[8]

[8] **St Paul**

Detail: bust
St Paul
(inner narthex, right side of the door leading into the nave)

In late Byzantine church decorations, the placing of the two 'princes' of the apostles, Ss Peter and Paul, at each side of the door to the nave, is frequently encountered. Paul stands in a three-quarters pose, facing the door and his companion; he raises his right hand in the gesture of teaching, the tip of the ring finger touching the tip of the thumb. In his left hand the closed codex of his epistles is seen (omitted in the picture). As in representations of the apostles, he wears a blue tunic with a red clavus and a violet himation. His features are traditional; a long, ovoid head to express his profound intellect, a lofty furrowed forehead with wrinkles, the scant hair, the rather pointed beard and a hooked nose.

11

[9] The Enthroned Christ and the Donor
*Jesus Christ, the dwelling-place of the living
The Founder, the Logothete of the Genikon,
Theodore Metochites
(inner narthex, above the entrance to the nave)*

The position of the mosaic confirms the Byzantine tradition of putting the donor image above the entrance to the nave. In the centre, Christ is seen seated in a nearly frontal pose on a jewelled throne. Two cushions are seen on the throne. His feet rest on a footstool, His left hand tightly holds the closed Book of the Gospels and His right hand is raised in a gesture of blessing. To the left, kneeling and offering his church to Christ, is Theodore Metochites, 'founder' of the monument. He is drawn traditionally without any reference to his real physique. He wears a dress like a kaftan, and a fashionable hat which brings to mind a turban. His hat was known as a 'skiadion' (literally, sunshade) and the outer garment as the 'kabbadion'. The model church in his hands is a simplified version of the Chora with the parecclesion omitted. He gives the impression of being squeezed into the left corner. This lack of balance can be anything but a mistake on the part of the artist. This tendency of asymmetry and imbalance is evident in many panels of the Chora. The title of Metochites meant being the controller of the general treasury of the Byzantine state and chief minister to the emperor. As a scholar and politician, Metochites was one of the most important men of his time. Shortly after restoring the Chora, Emperor Andronikos II made him Grand Logothete. However, after the fall of Andronikos II, he was sent into exile. A few years before he died, he was allowed to return to Constantinople where he lived in the Chora as a monk.

[10] The Deesis
Detail: the Virgin
[11] The Deesis
Detail: Christ Chalkites

[12] The Genealogy of Christ
(inner narthex, fourth bay, southern dome)
medallion
Jesus Christ

upper zone
From Adam to

Jacop	*Jared*	*Saruch*	*Phalec*
Adam	*Lamech*	*Nachor*	*Ragau*
Seth	*Sem*	*Thara*	*Enoch*
Noah	*Japheth*	*Abraham*	*Enos*
Cainan	*Japheth*	*Isaac*	*Abel*
Maleleel	*Arphaxand*	*Jacob*	

lower zone
The Sons of Jacob, Two Sons of Judah, and the Son of Pharez

Reuben ⎤
Simeon
Levi ⎟ *by Leah*
Judah
Zebulun
Isachar ⎦

Dan by Bilhah
Gad ⎤ *by Zilpah*
Asher ⎦
Naphtali by Bilhah
Joseph ⎤ *by Rachel*
Benjamin ⎦

   In one of his writings, the founder of the Chora, Theodore Metochites says that his purpose in decorating the Chora is 'to relate in mosaic and paintings how the Lord Himself . . . became a mortal on our behalf'. Thus he gives a clue to the iconographic programme of the decoration of the Chora. This iconographic programme, except for a few points, is on the whole conservative. For Theodore Metochites, there was one area in which not only originality, but even involvement was to be avoided: the area of theology. The starting point of the programme of the mosaics is the southern dome of the inner narthex. Together with the northern dome of the inner narthex, both domes are the highly decorative kind known as fluted, or melon. Though they are very much alike in construction, they differ perceptibly in size, in the number of flutes and windows, and in the patterns and prevailing colours of their ornamentation. While the diameter of the southern dome is 3.74 m, that of the northern dome is 3.40 m. The southern dome was constructed with 24 flutes and 9 windows. At its summit Christ Pantokrator is seen. In this dome, the large number of figures required the flutes to be very narrow and semicircular. Altogether 66 portraits of ancestors are placed in the flutes of the domes; 39 of these in the two zones of the southern dome represent the genealogy of Christ from Adam to Esrom. Some of these figures bear iconographic significance. Noah carries the ark, a symbol from the beginning of Christian art which recalls the hope of salvation from the deluge of sin.

[13] The Genealogy of Christ
(inner narthex, first bay, northern dome)

medallion
Mother of God

upper zone
Kings of the House of David: David to Salathiel

David	*Joatham*
Solomon	*Acnaz*
Roboam	*Ezekias*
Abia	*Manasses*
Asa	*Amon*
Josaphat	*Josias*
Joram	*Jechonias*
Ozias	*Salathiel*

lower zone
'Other Ancestors outside the Genealogy'

Hananiah	*Aaron*
Azariah	*Hur*
Mishael	*Samuel*
Daniel	*Job*
Johua	*Melchizedek*
Moses	

In the upper zone of the northern dome 16 kings of Judah, beginning with David, are portrayed. The group of figures in the lower zone is not strictly speaking in the lineage of Christ, but they are nevertheless, regarded as 'other ancestors who are outside the genealogy' because they were thought to have foretold the Incarnation. The northern dome was constructed with 16 flutes and 5 windows. Since the number of flutes is less than that of the southern dome, here the flutes are wider and shallower. The corresponding of the number of the figures in the ancestry to the number of flutes in the northern and southern domes is not accidental. Study of the iconographic programme of the mosaics of the Chora has shown that prior to the construction of the narthexes the general outline of the iconographic programme of the decoration of the building must have been formulated.

[14] The Annunciation to St Anne
Detail: Anne and the angel
St Anne praying in the garden
(inner narthex, first bay, eastern lunette)

[15] The Birth of the Virgin
Detail: preparation of the bath
The birth of the Theotokos
(inner narthex, second bay, eastern lunette)

In the panel, in accordance with the customs of the time, the mosaicist has gathered all the motifs encountered in Christ's nativity. A maid and midwife are seen preparing the bath of the newly-born Mary. She is rendered as a charming and robust infant. This tendency is common for all the other representations of babies in the Chora. They are always drawn very robust and healthy, almost Herculean. While the midwife holds her, the servant pours water into her bath. Although rendering in profile was a technique in which medieval artists, including those of the Chora, very often failed, both of these figures are successfully drawn in profile. Joachim is represented peering out of a doorway. A woman is seen wielding a fan of peacock feathers on a pole, and three young female figures approach the mother bearing gifts. In the picture only one of them is included. The offering of gifts at birth is a common theme and observed often in the birth of Greek gods and heroes.

[16] The First Seven Steps of the Virgin
She who takes seven steps
(inner narthex, transverse arch between the second and third bays, eastern soffit)

The theme of the mosaic derives from the Protevangelium 6:1: 'And day by day the child waxed strong, and when she was six months old her mother stood her upon the ground to try if she would stand, and she walked seven steps and returned to her bosom'. The First Steps is an old and popular theme found in the legend of Buddha or Indians of North America. The blown scarf is the most interesting feature of the scene and it is often found in the pagan art of late classical antiquity, mostly in mosaic pavements. It is one of the examples which shows the interest of the artists and patrons of the Palaiologian era in ancient models. The baby's eagerness to reach her mother without falling is caught admirably. This mosaic panel is one of two instances in the Chora where the natural colour of the stone tesserae was changed by application of pigments. After the building in the background was made of grey stones in order to give depth to the surface and create different surfaces, different values of dull reddish-brown pigment were applied to the mosaic. The original colour of the mosaic surface is left on the faces of the building which are parallel to the picture plane.

[17] The Presentation of the Virgin in the Temple
Detail: the Holy of Holies
The Holy of Holies
(inner narthex, third bay, vault)

The scene of the Virgin's presentation in the temple derives from the account of the Protevangelium 6:2: 'And the child became three years old, and Joachim said: Call the daughters of the Hebrews that are undefiled, and let them take every one, one lamp and let them be burning. . . . And the priest received her and kissed her. . . . And made her to sit upon the third step of the altar'. Zacharias (father of John the Baptist) is seen with arms extended to receive the Virgin before the gate of the temple. Joachim and Anne urge their daughter to advance toward the high priest. Another independent composition, the Virgin Fed by an Angel, is incorporated in this scene. Mary is represented sitting under the ciborium on the third step of a platform — not the altar. She extends one hand to receive the loaf of bread from the angel who is seen entering from the left.

[18] The Presentation of the Virgin in the Temple
Detail: two attendants

[16]

[19] The Virgin Receiving the Skein of Purple Wool

Detail: priests and architecture
The servants having brought the wool for the virgins to take, the purple fell to Mary's lot.
(inner narthex, second bay, western lunette)

The composition depicting this theme is not often encountered in mosaic art. Its rarity and the extensive treatment of the subject makes the composition in the Chora very unusual. According to the account of Protevangelium, Chapter 10: 'Now there was a council of the temple of the Lord. And the priest said: Call unto me pure virgins of the tribe of David. . . . And they brought them into the temple of the Lord, and the priest said: Cast me lots, which of you shall weave the gold and the undefiled and the fine linen and the silk and the hyacinthine, and the scarlet and the true purple. And the lot of the true purple and the scarlet fell unto Mary. . . . ' The falling of the royal colours to Mary distinguishes her as one from whom the prophesied Messiah was to spring. In this mosaic however, the skein is red, not purple.

[20] The Virgin Entrusted to Joseph

Detail: Zacharias and Mary
The handing over to Joseph
(inner narthex, second bay, western lunette)

'And when he took the rods and went forth and gave them back to them: and there was no sign upon them. But Joseph received the last rod: and lo, a dove, came forth of the rod and flew upon the head of Joseph. And the priest said unto Joseph: Unto thee hath it fallen to take the Virgin of the Lord and keep her thyself. And Joseph refused saying: I have sons and I am an old man, she is but a girl: lest I become the laughing-stock of the children of Israel'. Zacharias is depicted in a protective gesture with one hand resting on the head of Mary and the other holding the rod of Joseph. Around the knob of the rod a few green leaves are seen. In similar compositions of the same event in Mary's life, either the dove or the rod are used. The use of only the flowering rod as in the Chora is rare.

[21] Joseph Taking the Virgin to his House

Detail: Mary, Joseph, and a son of Joseph
Joseph, taking the Theotokos, goes to his house
(inner narthex, transverse between the first and second bays, western half)

This is a rarely depicted subject. The Protevangelium merely says: 'And Joseph was afraid, and took her to keep her for himself'. In the mosaic, Mary, Joseph and one of Joseph's sons are seen walking to the right away from a building which fills the background, which must be the temple. Mary is represented with her covered hands held up before her. Joseph is drawn walking to the right, but with his head not only in profile but turned 180º backward. He looks back at Mary. In order to indicate the rapid pace of the figures, the drapery around the feet of Joseph and Mary is drawn in an agitated manner.

[22] The Annunciation of the Virgin at the Well

The annunciation at the well
(outer narthex, first bay, southwestern pendentive)

According to the narrative of the Protevangelium 11:1 Mary 'took the pitcher and went forth to fill it with water: and lo a voice saying: Hail, thou that art highly favoured, the Lord is with thee, blessed art thou among women. And she looked about her upon the right hand and upon the left to see whence the voice should be'. The mosaicist has caught the moment of surprise successfully. As she bends to the well Mary is startled by the voice of the angel, who is depicted approaching the scene from the right.

[23] The Enrolment for Taxation

Detail: Mary

Mary is depicted as an unusually tall figure. She stands erect, her head bowed toward the officers; with the right hand she draws her maphorion about her shoulders. Her other hand is hidden in her drapery. She is represented 'great with child'.

[20]

[24] The Enrolment for Taxation

Mother of God

. . . because he was of the house and lineage of David . . . To be taxed with Mary his espoused wife, being great with child.

(outer narthex, first bay, eastern lunette)

As is often observed in the mosaics and frescoes of the Chora, the important figures, here Cyrenius and Mary, are given prominence by being drawn bigger than the others and by being placed symmetrically in front of the vertical elements, two tower-like buildings. At the centre of the scene, the scribe holding an unfurled scroll on which he inscribes the names, and a guard holding a sheathed sword in his left hand are seen.

[26]

[25] Herod Ordering the Massacre of the Innocents
Detail: a mother
(outer narthex, sixth bay, eastern lunette)

The scene is one of the finest in the Chora. The artist has achieved the dramatic effect of the moment of despair not only through the voluminous aspect of the mother's garments, but also through her pose, extended arms and tangled hair. To these he has added the contrasting colours of mosaic cubes.

[26] The Mothers Mourning for their Children
Detail: a group of mothers
In Rome was there a voice heard, lamentation, and weeping, and great mourning.
(outer narthex, fifth bay, western lunette)

The theme of mourning mothers is treated elaborately in the Chora and a separate lunette is reserved for it. Unfortunately only the right side has survived to the present day. The composition is based on the account of Matthew (2:17, 18): 'Then was fulfilled that which was spoken by Jeremy the prophet, saying, in Rama was there a voice heard, lamentation, and weeping, and great mourning, Rachel weeping for the children, and would not be comforted, because they are not'. In the fragment which survives, a group of silently crying mothers are seen huddled together in various attitudes of sorrow. Their faces reflect deep grief. One of them raises her right hand to her face and holds the severed head of her child in the other. At the right corner, another mother holding her dead child is depicted. The heads of all of the mothers are turned to the left, towards the missing section of the mosaic. In the missing part of the composition there must have been a scene of horror, an executioner, Herod, or perhaps the pile of dead children.

[27] The Miracle at Cana
(outer narthex, third bay, vault, northern half)

Christ stands with a scroll in His left hand and His right hand extended towards the tumbler offered to Him. Mary is partly obscured by the halo and figure of her son. Her role in the miracle was an important one, because it was she who instigated it and instructed the servants to obey Christ's orders. In the pendentive 6 pithoi, or earthenware jars are seen. They are made of terracotta tesserae, the material of which the jars themselves would have been made. A young man dressed in a short-sleeved tunic is seen pouring water into one of the jars from a golden vessel. At the far right another youth is seen approaching carrying a vessel. Behind the first youth the governor of the feast stands. He is represented as a bearded old man. He wears a blue, tight-sleeved tunic ornamented with gold and red at the cuffs, and a red mantle and a blue scarf.

[28] The Multiplication of Loaves
Detail: Christ giving bread to two disciples
(outer narthex, third bay, vault, southern half)

The four gospels agree upon the four episodes: 1. Christ took five loaves and, looking up to heaven, He blessed them; 2. Christ broke the bread and gave it to His disciples; 3. The disciples in turn, redistributed it to the multitude (5,000 men besides women and children); 4. After the multitude had eaten, the disciples 'took up the fragments that remained, twelve baskets full' (Matt. 14:20). Christ is seen close to three baskets filled with broken pieces of bread. In each hand He holds bread and is about to give it to the disciples who stand with hands extended to receive it. The older disciple is Philip who is often represented as a beardless young man. Here he is replaced by an older man with a short beard. The two disciples are about to receive the bread from the hands of Christ. At the right, a part of the waiting multitude, a mother with her child standing on her lap and a few people are seen. In this panel after the mosaic tesserae had been set, in order to make the baskets stand out more prominently from the similar brown colour of the background, and to sharpen the contrast between the pieces of bread and their background, brown pigment was applied. In all the mosaics of the Chora except for the scene of the First Seven Steps of the Virgin, this is the only case of colour correction by the use of pigments.

[29] Christ Healing Two Blind Men
Detail: the blind men
Christ healing the two blind men
Jesus Christ
(inner narthex, fourth bay, northwestern pendentive)

From the left, followed by two of His disciples (omitted in the picture) Christ approaches two young blind men seated under a tree outside the walls of Jericho. His arm is extended in blessing. In His left hand He holds a scroll. The first of the blind youths holds the end of a long staff in his left hand and gestures towards Christ with his right. The second one who in seated nearest to the tree, extends both hands in supplication to the 'Son of David' (Matt. 20:30, 31). The youths are dressed in simple tunics. A gnarled tree springing out horizontally to shelter the blind men leans to the left. Its foliage is rendered in blue glass tesserae and it bears white fruit.

[30] Christ Healing the Leper
Detail: the leper
Christ healing the leper
Jesus Christ
(inner narthex, fourth bay, western side of the southern arch)

The figure of the leper has survived almost intact. His only garment is a loincloth tied in front. His body is rendered in light grey and yellow stones, and his spots in dull brown porous stone.

[29]

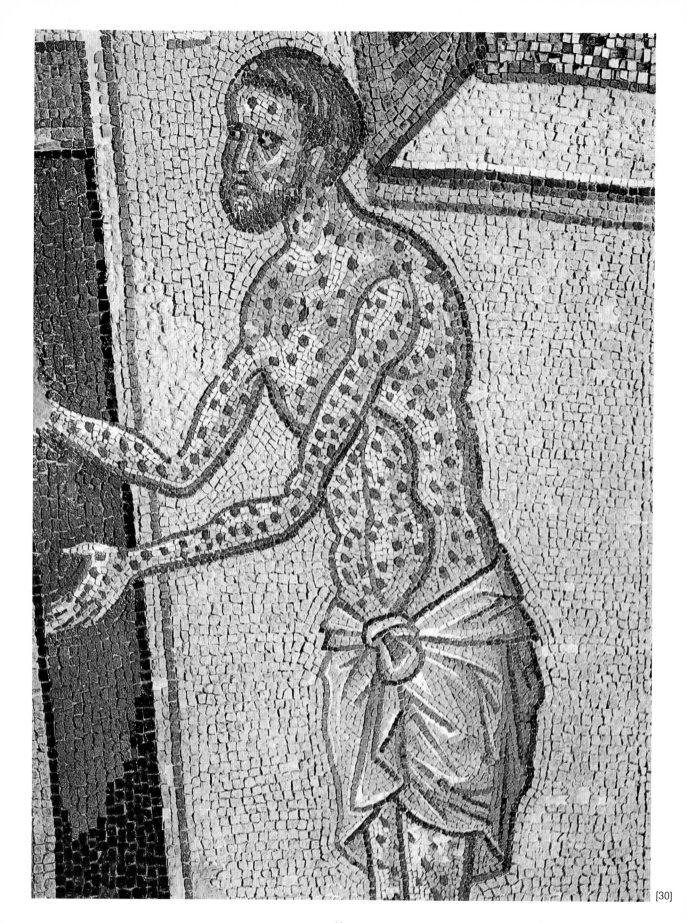

[30]

[31]

[31] **The Dormition of the Virgin**

The Dormition of the Theotokos
Jesus Christ
(west wall of the nave above the entrance door)

Owing probably to its strong marble frame, this mosaic is one of the best preserved in the Chora. It was discovered in 1920. Theotokos is the popular name for the Mother of God in eastern Christion countries. To fit in all the figures related to the event, the mosaicist has used a triangular setting. The Virgin, who is represented stretched out on a bed, forms the lower edge of the triangle. In the outer zone of the almond-shaped triangle the angels are represented. Christ is seen turning slightly toward the right, but His face is turned in the other direction, toward that of His mother. The figure of the soul of Mary sits in His hands.

[32] **Parecclesion. Looking east**

THE PARECCLESION

Like the narthexes, the parecclesion was a new construction added to the building by Theodore Metochites. It consists of two square bays and an apse separated from each other by transverse arches. The sanctuary of the parecclesion consists of an arch and an apse covered by a semidome. This section served a liturgical purpose as in a church. The vaults of the two bays of the parecclesion have four recessed niches altogether which were built within the thickness of the walls for tombs. Its second bay is covered by a domical vault. The dome is carried by a drum on pendentives and it contains 12 ribs and 12 windows. Stylistic and practical considerations suggest that the frescoes in the parecclesion were painted after the mosaics had been completed, very probably in the years 1320–21. However, the funerary paintings of the wall tombs must have been executed later at different times when the need for them arose. The frescoes of the parecclesion were uncovered by the Byzantine Institute between 1951 and 1958.

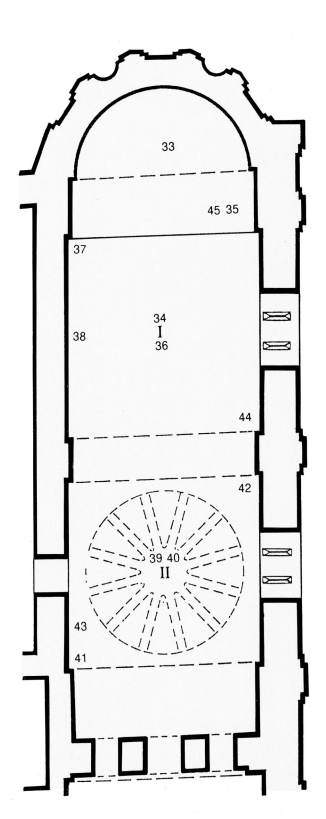

Plan of the parecclesion and key numbers of the location of the frescoes included in this volume

[33] The Anastasis
[34] The Last Judgement
[35] The Raising of the Daughter of Jairus
[36] The Last Judgement
[37] The Last Judgement
[38] The Last Judgement
[39] The Virgin and Child and Attendant Angels
[40] The Virgin and Child and Attendant Angels
[41] Four Hymnographers (St Theophanes)
[42] Four Hymnographers (St Cosmas)
[43] Jacob's Ladder; Jacob Wrestling with the Angel
[44] The Bearing of the Ark of the Covenant
[45] The Virgin Eleousa

[33] The Anastasis
The resurrection
Jesus Christ
(apse, semidome)

The essential points of the narrative which deal with this theme relate that John the Baptist enters hell and announces to the righteous (the forefathers and prophets) that Christ has sent him to announce His coming that they may be saved. Satan commands Hades to hold Christ fast when He comes, and he warns him of Christ's power to raise the dead and deprive him of his captives. Hades orders his devils to make fast the gates of brass and bars and locks of iron. Upon Christ's command the gates are broken and the dead are loosened from their bonds. Then He raises Adam as a sign of redemption of all the righteous.

In the Chora, either because of the apse, where the scene was seldom placed, or to emphasize Christ's neutrality towards the sexes, Eve is also included in the scene. Christ, as the vanquisher of death, is represented in an active movement contrasting with the passive rendering of the figures of Adam and Eve. On the left John the Baptist, and on the right Abel are seen. Under the feet of Christ are the two leaves of the broken gates of hell with their hinges and keys, and Satan is seen with his feet tightly fettered and his wrists bound behind him in manacles joined to an iron collar around his neck by a long bar of iron.

[34] **The Last Judgement**
Detail: the Scroll of Heaven
(first bay, vault, centre)

An angel is seen in the act of rolling up the scroll of heaven. The unfurled portion of the scroll is formed into a spiral, like an Ionic volute, and on it the sun, the moon and stars are depicted. The sun bears the features of a face which emits rays. In the volute, eight-pointed stars are seen. The scene must have been inspired by the description in the Apocalypse 6:14 'And the heaven departed as a scroll when it is rolled together' and in Matt. 24:29: 'the sun shall be darkened, and the moon shall not give her light . . . ' before the Second Coming of Christ.

[35] The Raising of the Daughter of Jairus
(arch of the bema, south side)

This fresco is a good example of the arrangement of the figures in an architectural setting in the mosaics and frescoes of the Chora. Christ and his followers — Peter, James, John and three unidentifiable saints, are placed in front of a tower-like structure on the left side. Opposite them in front of another tower is the second group: the daughter of Jarius, her parents and two more attendants. The daughter of Jairus has just been restored to life and is seen sitting upright on her bed. A wall joins the two towers and achieves a degree of horizontality in the predominantly vertical composition. This is a very familiar combination in Byzantine art. The roofs of the towers are joined by long red drapery. These elements are often observed in the mosaics and frescoes of the Chora and do not necessarily indicate an outdoor scene. They are imaginative and merely decorative. The scene is to be imagined as taking place in an interior. Among the colour treatment of the frescoes in the Chora, that of the mantles of the women at the far right deserves to be emphasized. The darker areas are painted in reddish and yellowish browns, the fully-lighted areas in complimentary light blue, to give the effect of 'shot' or changeable colour.

[36] The Last Judgement
The Deesis
(first bay, vault, east side)

The Second Coming Choir of Hierarchs Choir of Holy Men   Choir of (Holy) Women Choir of Martyrs   Choir of Apostles   Choir of Prophets Come, ye blessed of my Father, inherit the kingdom prepared for you from the foundation of the world. Depart from me, ye cursed, into everlasting fire, prepared for the devil and his angels.

The fresco shows Christ's description of His Second Coming as it is described in Matt. 25:31: 'When the Son of Man shall come in His glory, and all the holy angels with Him, then shall He sit upon the throne of His glory'. The 'throne' was originally a narrow arch which has survived on the left. The mandorla of Christ was made of four shades of blue, the darkest being at the centre. His wounded hands are extended to make gestures of acceptance and rejection. His dress must have once been covered with gold leaf, which has still partly survived in the halo around His head. The inscription ICXC is divided into two by the halo. The figures of the Virgin and John the Baptist complete the scene. In the background, holding pearl-studded sceptres, angels are seen.

[37] The Last Judgement
Lazarus the Beggar in Abraham's Bosom.
Detail: souls to the right of Abraham
(first bay, vault, northeastern pendentive)

[38] The Last Judgement
The Entry of the Elect into Paradise
Detail: Apostles, the Gate of Paradise, the Good Thief
(first bay, northern lunette)

St Peter is seen about to insert a key into the lock of Paradise. A group of Elect follows him. A Cherub holding a sword which is pointed downward guards the gate. Inside the gate the Good Thief, clad only in a loincloth and holding a wooden cross, is seen.

[39] The Virgin and Child and attendant Angels
Detail: the fifth angel
(second bay, dome)

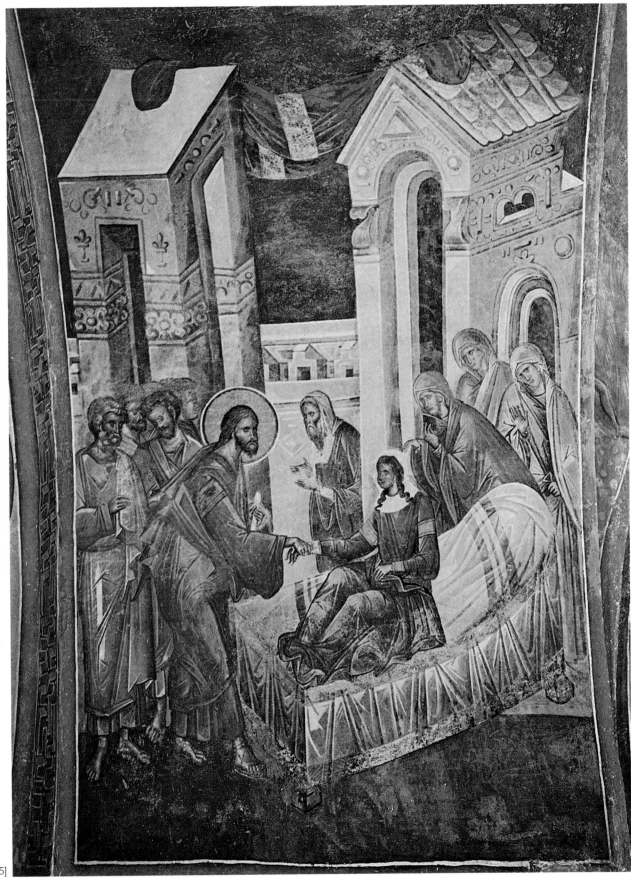

[40] The Virgin and Child and Attendant Angels

Detail: the Virgin and Child
(second bay, dome, summit)

Mother of God
Angel of the Lord
(above each of the twelve angels)

The second bay of the parecclesion deals with the Virgin, and Old Testament subjects which prefigured her role in the divine plan of salvation. The dome of the bay is pierced by 12 windows. Its 12 ribs converge in the summit where a medallion of the Virgin and Child is placed. The medallion is similar in type to the mosaic medallion in the summit of the northern dome of the inner narthex. The Child is dressed in a golden tunic and a 'himation'. He holds out His hands at each side and makes a sign of blessing with them. The Virgin is clad in a deep blue-violet tunic and mantle, and her head is covered by a maphorion which has a golden fringe. At each shoulder there is a golden eight-pointed star with a dot at the centre. In the ribs of the dome, the angels and archangels who worship the incarnate Christ and His mother, the instruments of Incarnation, are placed (omitted in the picture). The angels are clothed brilliantly in a fanciful court attire of 6 separate items.

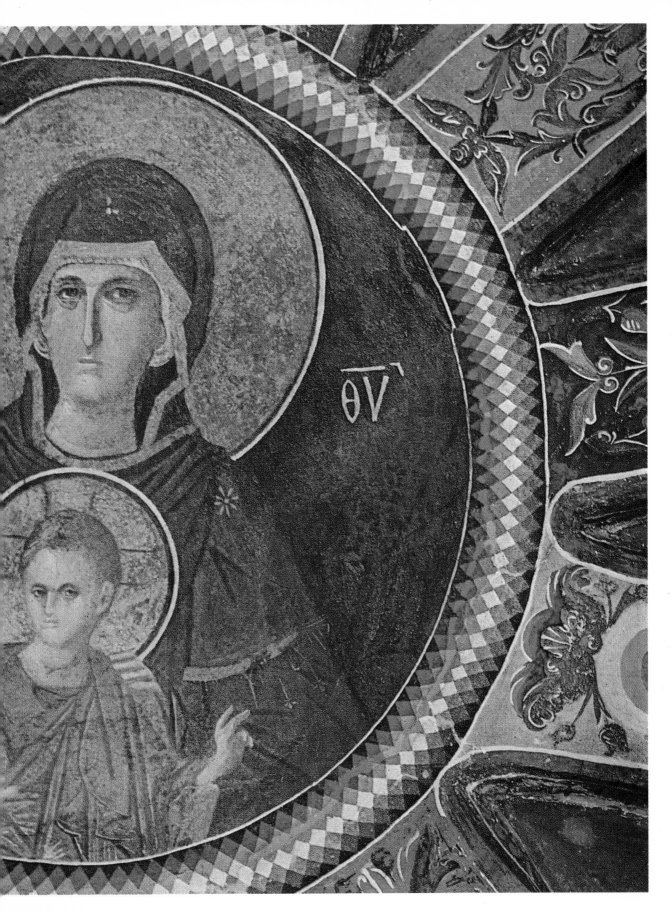

[41] **Four Hymnographers**
Detail: St Theophanes, hymnographer.
St Theophanes
We were turned back to the earth after having transgressed God's divine commandment . . .
(second bay, northwestern pendentive)

[42] **Four Hymnographers**
Detail: St Cosmas, hymnographer
(second bay, southeastern pendentive)

The four poet-hymnographers are portrayed in the act of composition. They bring to mind the Four Evangelists. They are dressed in monastic garb and are seen bent toward their work. The other two hymnographers portrayed in the pendentives are St John of Damascene and St Joseph the Poet. The writings in their notebooks are deciphered as *What joy of life remains without its share of sorrow . . . and Propitiation of the world, spotless Virgin*, respectively.

[43] **Jacob's Ladder; Jacob Wrestling with the Angel**
(second bay, northern lunette, western half)

Mother of God
And Jacob took one of the stones of the place and put it at his head, and lay down to sleep...
. . . in that place, and dreamed
. . . and behold a ladder fixed on the earth, whose top reached heaven and the angels of God ascended and descended on it. And the Lord stood upon it.

In the lower section of the scene the youthful Jacob is represented asleep on the ground (in the picture only his legs and feet are seen). Above him there is a great curved flight of stairs. Four angels are depicted ascending or descending on the stairs. At the top of the stairs the Virgin and Child are represented (omitted in the picture). At the right, Jacob and the angel are depicted locked in their struggle. In the course of this event he saw 'God face to face' (Gen. 28:10-17) and was touched in the hollow of his thigh, and was renamed (Gen. 32:24-30).

[44] **The Bearing of the Ark of the Covenant**
And it came to pass when Solomon had built the house of the Lord, then he assembled the elders of Israel in Sion that they might bring up the ark of the covenant of the Lord out of the city of David, which is Sion. And the priests took up the ark of the covenant of the Lord and the tabernacle of testimony.
(second bay, southern lunette, eastern half)

The ark and holy vessels were kept in the tabernacle within the fortress of Zion which was also known as the city of David, until Solomon constructed the temple. Four priests are represented carrying the ark of the covenant, which is rendered like a sarcophagus on their shoulders. A section of the scene in the southern pendentive is included in the upper right corner of the picture. It is from the Apocalypse 20:13, the Land and Sea Giving their Dead. In the picture, human bodies, heads and feet are seen emerging from the mouths of fish.

Ὁ Ἅ ΘΕΟΦΆΝΗС

Ὁ Ἅ(ΓΙΟϹ) ΚΟϹΜᾶς Ὁ ΠΟΙΗΤ(ΗϹ)

[44]

[45]

[45] **The Virgin Eleousa**
Mother of God
Jesus Christ
(arch of the bema, southern end)

Originally, opposite this scene at the northern end of the arch of the bema, Christ must have been depicted. The full-length standing type of the Virgin is known as the Eleousa (the Merciful, or Compassionate). This painting of the Virgin must have been venerated as an icon because two points on the footstool show discolouration, which must have been caused by the heat and smoke of votive lamps or candles.

[48]

[46] **Exterior view from the east**

[47], [48], [49], [50], [51] **The wooden houses near the Chora**

The quarter of İstanbul in which the Chora is located is one of the most interesting of the old city. When the church was turned into a mosque in the sixteenth century it was named Kariye Cami, the word Kariye in Arabic incidentally, meaning 'countryside' like the Greek word 'chora'. When the traveller enters any of the narrow side streets approaching the present museum, he is often accompanied by hordes of friendly children, and followed by the inquisitive looks of their mothers through embroidered white curtains. The day's laundry hangs from the balconies of wooden houses. It is to Çelik Gülersoy, the director of the Touring and Automobile Club of Turkey, that we owe the existence of the present surroundings of the Chora. If it had not been for his endless efforts to protect these houses, by now they would have either fallen into ruin or been engulfed by ugly blocks of concrete apartments. The wooden houses, the people who live in them, the cafe-restaurant, the Ottoman fountain and the gardens laid out behind the site, have become inseparable parts of the Chora following the restorations. After a visit to the Chora, the more enthusiastic sightseers can walk within a short distance along the impressive walls of Theodosius II, to the palace of Porphyrogenitus, built in the twelfth century by Emperor Manuel I. It is commonly known as 'Tekfur Sarayı'. Unfortunately, having fallen into ruins, the sole existing example of Byzantine secular architecture, the palace, does not get the attention which it really deserves. The Theodosian walls considered in medieval times as an additional wonder of the world, stretch from the Marmara Sea in the south and link with the sea walls of the Golden Horn in the north, a distance of approximately 9 kilometres. These extraordinary ramparts, completed in the incredibly short space of 12 months, were razed by a disastrous earthquake just before the time when the army of Atilla, the Hun, was advancing rapidly through Thrace. Fortunately, the Byzantines were able to rebuild the walls in two months and added an outer wall in front, complete with moat and towers.

[49]

[50]

[51]